# The Unexpected

# Journey

## Esther Beautiful

BookLeaf
Publishing

The Unexpected Journey © 2023 Esther Beautiful

Presentation by *BookLeaf Publishing*

Web: www.bookleafpub.com

E-mail: info@bookleafpub.com

ISBN: 9789358367430

First edition 2023

*This book is dedicated to someone who supported me, believed in me, encouraged me and was always there for me. He loved me no matter what. Rest in heaven, Damone.*

# ACKNOWLEDGEMENT

My thanks will always be to God who gave me the gift to express myself through words. However, I also thank the people who loved me and the people who hurt me. Without intense feelings, I'd have nothing to write.

# PREFACE

Enjoy the journey...

# A Gift

Small.
Beautiful.
Full of promise.
Endless possibilities.
Unexpected.
Exciting.
Heart racing...
I wonder...

(The Gift)
Do you really want to know
what's inside of me?
I could be everything
that you've ever hoped for.

I could make
your world go 'round.
I could bring you joy
like you've never known.

But what if I'm not
all of those things?
What if I'm not
what you expected?

Will you dash me
upon the ground?
Will you set me on a shelf
only to be forgotten?

Will you know what to do with me
once you received me?
Or will you be disappointed
because I'm not all that you had hoped I would
be?

Will you treat me with less regard
because I wasn't what you had expected?
Will you love me less over the years
when I'm no longer new?

Or will I become like a treasured childhood toy
that you will never let go?
Do you love me because of the anticipation?
The wonder?

Will the excitement subside
once you know what's inside?
Do you really
want to know?

Please do not open me...
unless you are prepared to accept me.
You cannot change what you find.

I am what I am.

Are you ready?

# Untamed Spirit

Beautiful. Exotic.
Yet unaware.
What is it about you
that makes you so different?
What is it about you
that catches my eye?
Why do I need you here with me,
in my life?
Entranced by your beauty.
Intrigued by your thoughts.
Amazed by your multiple facets.
I want to have you.
I want to keep you,
under my lock and key,
in a place,
where there will be no others,
who can take you away from me.
But like a bird
found in the wild,
You just cannot be caged.
For you would lose the beauty
that I've come to admire,
The oddness that makes you YOU.
The exceptional things
that make you different,

And the reasons why I love you.
So, precariously I hold onto
the moments that I have,
And hope beyond measure
to keep you.
Wild.
Untamed.
And with me.

# The Lonely Jar

It stands alone
on the middle
of the table
Flanked on either side
by nothing
Nearly overflowing.
As I pass it by
I place in another
penny
as my thoughts
pause to linger
on your pillow-soft kisses
and ponder the fireworks
that sound
in my ear
until the memory
trails into silence
and the lonely jar
reappears.
Filled past the brim
with pennies
for each time
my thoughts
journeyed
back to you.

# Wistful Yearning

Snowflakes whispering
    drifting restlessly
        whirring and gasping
            thru the distant sky.
        fluttering,
     wafting,
   melting
      into a bowl
       of tears.

# Evidence of You

Yesterday
a stranger
nameless
quiet
bold

Today
crinkly eyes
beautiful smile
joyful laughter
soothing sound

aggravating confidence
stubborn composure
adamant declarations

lovable annoyance
alluring banter
playful tease

Tomorrow
a mystery
but
nonetheless
a poem
in me

# Exquisite Flower

Exotic. Beautiful. Coveted.
High maintenance. Special soil.
Water daily. Extra care.
Keep shaded- well protected.
Gentle handling- mends slowly.
Keep potted- fragile roots.
Patience- blooms slowly.
Cost- expensive.
Satisfaction- guaranteed.

# Bereavement

Smiling destitute.
Spirited void.
Blessed anguish.
Generous vacancy.
Laughing misery.
Jubilant suffering.
Triumphant injury.

# Unspoken

I never stop to examine
the feelings that I have.
And should I?
If times were different,
If lines could be crossed,
Would we?
If I had known you sooner,
Would things be different
from what they are today?
How is it that you know me,
When you've never even known me?
And yet you do?
Why is it
that when I look at you
I can read your eyes
when your lips say something different?
Though you never say to me
the things that are on my mind,
I can hear you.
And I listen.
There are things I want to tell you,
things I want to share,
But I have boundaries.
There are things that you are thinking,
things I want to hear,

But you have boundaries.
It's enough for me
just to see you everyday.
I look at you.
You look at me.
And we've shared.
Unspoken.

# Baobab Tree

It stands alone on the African plain,
branches spread far and wide.
Where birds choose to build their nests
and insects live inside.
Impalas dancing in its shade.
Ground squirrels sleep in the root.
Monkeys swing from branch to branch
and baboons eat the fruit.
Leaves eaten by elephants.
Limbs for snakes to snooze.
Bark to make our instruments.
There's no part we can't use.
Bushbabies pluck the flowers.
Chameleons search for flies.
Leopards laying quietly
but no one hears the cries.
Will someone stop to listen,
to really look and see?
There's so much more to take away
from this majestic tree.
This tree should be embraced,
for the beauty it exudes.
Loved for the peacefulness
and joy that it renews.
Majestic and alone it stands,

This selfless, beautiful tree.
It is called the baobab.
The baobab is me.

# My Yes and Yes

When you look at me and ask
how was my day,
Do you believe me?
If I smile and say
that I'm doing okay,
Are you convinced?
Do you know the difference
between my yes and my yes?
Or do you accept the surface?
Can you sense the turmoil
that might be brewing
beneath my joyful demeanor?
People hurt you
and never see
the scars they've left behind.
They tread on you
like boats on water
ripping through the bay.
On the surface,
rolling water,
beauty to the eye.
Underneath it
currents rupture.
Chaos. Chaos. Chaos.
But I'm okay.

That's what I'll say.
And never will you know.
Unless you learn
to sense the difference
between my yes and my yes.

# My Comforter

Swathed in my silky mink comforter,
I am sheltered and protected from the world.
Cozy and warm, I snuggle deeper
in search of passion and strength.
My comforter envelops me
in a consummate hold,
enduring, unremitting and tense.
I cling to my comforter
in search of security,
and it responds with a strong
and unyielding embrace.
It surrounds me with affection
and indulges me with warmth.
It suspends me
in a haven of love.
I am consoled.
I am relieved.
I am encouraged.
I am concealed
from the harshness and the pain.
Imparting with a sense of surety,
I emerge from the folds of my comforter,
armed with the knowledge that when I return,
I will be seized by its familiar embrace.

# Coveted Gift

You wanted me so bad that you could nearly
taste it.
Planning what you'd do with me.
Promising things you'd never fulfill.
You were so excited when you got me.
Eager.
Willing to please.
You treated me like precious china.
Protected.
Handled with care.
Displayed for all to see.
Until something else caught your fancy.
I was cast aside.
Abruptly.
Without care.
As you pursued another gift.
Something new.
But once that gift became old,
it was then that you realized my value.
That new gift-- it wasn't me.
Cheap.
Vain.
False.
Without substance.
Your needs were shaped when you chose me.

I'm the real thing,
and nothing
will ever
be better.

# Tranquility

with your mouth
you murdered me
you descended on me
violently
like judgment.
your frigid eyes clawing
 my skin
  ripping
   shredding
    slitting
     until nothing
      was left
       but remnants
        you scraped
         into a trivial heap.
          relentless ambushing
           your frothy mouth
            hurling venom
             as your voice
              blazed my residue.
             Blanketed by serenity
            I sat listening
           to soft rain drops
          echoing
         unruffled
       in my secret place.

# A Letter to Karma

I know she felt wronged
by the accident
blown by the sight
of her child.
The purple hues
of her injury
plunged her into a tirade
meant to strip me
of my dignity
and leave me
vulnerable
and demeaned.
There is nothing more I can do
to make it right.
I have apologized sincerely.
I cannot give any more of me.
And because of the way
she treated me,
I want to see to her consequence.
Capture her with tenderness.
Consume her with benevolence.
Detain her with pleasantries.
Ruin her with generosity.
Shower her ruthlessly
with favor and affection.

Slaughter her with bliss.
Then release her
with a measure
of love.

# I Rise

the rainwaters
crash down on me
without ceasing.
muddying the waters
around me
grieving
the ones I love
but my roots
are now shallow
like a dandelion weed.
I can not
be overturned.
I peer into the pools
surrounding me
and a reflection
of strength
stares back.
I rise up
from the depths
of depression.
I rise up
from the hatred
and pain.
I rise up
and I press thru

never ceasing
by dancing
and singing
His praise.

# Piercing Imprints

This journey has been painful,
But my God, He pulls me through,
Sometimes the tears are flowing
And there's nothing I can do.
Shards of glass lodged in my heart,
Escaping through my eyes,
Pooling on the paintings,
Created as disguise...
The beautiful conceptions
Birthed of hidden pain,
An inexplicable emotion
That I cannot restrain.
The loss of many loved ones,
Living and passed away,
Too much for me to handle,
All I do is pray.
Those who've gone before me,
I'll see again one day.
Those who are still living,
I love you anyway.
Despite the pain you cause me,
Although you stay apart,
The hurt cannot outweigh the love
I carry in my heart.

# I See You

I know how it feels to be the one
still here when you go away,
Crying through the night,
and crying through the day.

Left alone to face the world
and pick up all the pieces.
Our hearts are ripped and crumpled up,
We'll never smooth the creases.

You killed yourself to stop your pain
But we died that day too.
It made suicide an option
when there's pain we can't push through.

So now we live with suicide
and being suicidal.
The chains of death are wrapped too tight
and cannot be unbridled.

I also understand your hurt,
So much pain you want to die.
Death seems like the easy out
When no one hears your cry.

Agony, hopelessness,
Regret you can't explain,
The bravest thing you'll ever do
is live despite the pain.

# When Love is Hoarded

drowning in a pool of tears
with people all around,
gasping, stabbing, crumbling
until I heard a sound,
harmonious expressions,
spoken from her heart,
strengthening me, uplifting me
before I fell apart.
I thought I was invisible
but she could see my pain,
I wondered at the depth of hers
behind the smile she feigned
I began to watch her live her life,
I saw the love she gave,
always received so eagerly
for she offered it so brave
She loved without abandon
through gifts, through words, through deeds
Appreciated tremendously,
But no one met her needs
They happily received her love,
and they truly loved her too,
But never expressing the way they felt
until her time was due
Silently they stood there,

shuffling to the front,
remembering the pain she eased from them
and how she took the brunt
Remorseful and regretful,
Exploding from the pain,
Recalling all the memories
of the smiles she once feigned
If only someone had seen her,
If only they had come,
Her smile could be so genuine
and our hearts would not be numb
We left her there all alone
we took the love she had,
No one stopped to wonder
How she recognized the sad.
The same pain that we feel inside
when we feel as no one cares,
is the same pain that she recognized
and the same one that she bears.
We kept the love we have for her
We took the love she gave
All the love we held from her
are the tears shed at her grave.

# Life Without You

Pools of tears, vacant eyes,
Laughter disappeared.
Words mutated into gasps,
Heaving out the fears.
Body crumpled to the floor,
Collapsing in disbelief.
Jolted into emptiness,
And the weightiness of grief.
Hollow, Hollow, Hollowness,
Falling through the ground.
Melting into nothingness,
Never to be found.
Lost, alone, crestfallen,
Disheartened and depleted.
Isolated, broken down,
Cheated and defeated.

# Keep Turning the Page

story climaxing
page turning
you no longer there.
Emptiness
lies
before
me.
Where is up?
Where is down?
Where is forward?
standing frozen
alone
isolated
hollow
immobile
endless moments pass me by
breathing
eating
sleeping
living
in emptiness
unraveling
trembling
breaking
looking everywhere

looking anywhere
searching
searching for you
searching for me
searching for us
my eyes fall
upon a scarlet thread
and I pull it
and I pull it
and I pull it
the life that was
begins to fade
the scarlet thread
knitting into my now
stitching me back together
slowly
carefully
gently
shifting
shifting
shifting
finally
emerging
fragments of you
engrafted in me
intertwined
forever
turning the page
a little more ready

for the next time
emptiness
lies
before
me

# The Unexpected Journey

"I'm sorry,
he's deceased"
jolted me
into a tunnel
of unbelief
and I lay there
collapsed
on the floor.
Time ticking.
Heart beating.
Mouth breathing.
Dead.
Entombed by agony,
Tortured by despair,
Paralyzed by tragedy,
Lifeless.
Until the day
he said to me
"Keep going"
I could not see
in front of me,
Enveloped by
the blanket
of grief.
Blindly,

I reached out,
grasping desperately,
for anything.
Anything to ground me,
Anything to hold me,
Anything to keep me here.
I stumbled,
I trudged,
I waded,
through every
darkened sea.
Wave after wave
tried its best
to overtake me.
"Keep going"
I rested.
I cried.
I screamed.
I shouted.
Nothing brought
him back to me.
"Keep going"
A few steps forward,
another blow back.
"Keep going"
I want to die.
I want to curl up
on my couch
and never see

the light again.
"Keep going"
I don't know
where I am
anymore.
Plugging along
day by day...
"Keep going"
I want to quit now.
The pain is too much for me.
"Keep going"
I turn a corner
as I drag myself
into yet another week,
But this time
I notice
the load
is lighter.
I am breathing.
I am living.
I am laughing.
And I look back
from whence I came
and it dawns on me
that I made it
through the grief.
But my heart is saddened.
I've left you there.
Before I can tiptoe

into the darkness
once again,
I hear you.
"Keep going"
But this time
you're not in front of me.
You're inside of me.
I return to the path
you've paved with me
Stronger,
Resilient,
Wiser,
and I
keep going